GREAT
KIDS ROOMS

St. Martin's Press
New York

Library of Congress Cataloging in Publication Data

Weiss, Jeffrey.
  Great kids' rooms.

  1. Children's rooms. 2. Interior decoration.
I. Title.
NK2117.C4W4   747.7'7   81-5686
ISBN 0-312-34601-8 (pbk.)   AACR2

Printed in Hong Kong by The South China Printing Co.

GREAT
KIDS ROOMS

I remember, as a child, never feeling completely comfortable in my friends' bedrooms. Ricky's looked into the kitchen; the twins across the street shared a double bed wedged into a corner of the dining room; David's room was in the attic, through his older sisters' bedroom, and his ceiling sloped. Looking back on it, I suppose they felt queasy in mine which was on the first floor, looked into a hallway, and had a horizontal ceiling the way a bedroom should. But our childhood perceptions of what was proper and safe were formed, for the most part, by what we found familiar. In time, I slept overnight in their homes enough to learn the mysteries and commonplaces of their rooms: the peculiar and frightening way that light from the street crept across their ceilings at night, the sound of pipes knocking when the heat rose, the unique patter of raindrops off their gutters and the way the wind blew them against their window panes. David's bathroom always seemed too far away, though, and I was forever startled by the view of my own house from their windows.

Perhaps there was never really that much difference between our common experiences, no matter how we magnified them then. Ricky, David, the twins and all the others found retreats in their bedrooms, places of privacy and escape from their families. They all heard the commands "Go to your room!" when they were bad and "Clean up your room!" when their mothers thought it messy. They all managed to fall asleep in them at night, played games on the floors on rainy days and lay in their beds, staring at the dingy ceilings, whether straight or sloped, day after day, recovering from measles, chicken pox or mumps. We all had secret "things" hidden under our beds or in a carefully cluttered corner of the closet. Each of us proudly invited our friends, "Come see my room!"

My room! Even if we shared them with sisters or brothers or the dining room table, our children bedrooms were somehow always our private spaces. We went to them to play, sleep, think, read, brood, pout and plot. We knew the cracks in the ceilings, named the knots in the pine, fingered the bubbles in the plaster—aberrations closer and more faithful than cloud formations in the sky, familiar shapes of grotesque monsters and goblins that eventually became our friends, welcomed us home from the real world of school and afternoon jobs, shared their elfscapes with us when we were sick and sometimes frightened us at night. But they were always there. We wore ourselves out daydreaming, fantasizing these nooks and crannies of our bedrooms into pirate dens, palaces or enchanted gardens, shuffling furniture around, squeezing out every inch of privacy and secrecy that we could, overlaying our own visions on whatever decor our parents had provided for us. Ultimately, of course, we triumphed over our parents' imaginations and conquered our rooms because, as Longfellow said, a child's will "is the wind's will, and the thoughts of youth are long, long thoughts."

Today, our thoughts as adults have "shortened," our wills are held hostage by time, money, space, architects, child psychologists, toy designers, other hip and modern parents and the latest theory of heredity vs. environment. Like trolls, they invade the child's room and lurk in the shadowy corners, suggesting how it ought to be. The room. Yet we cannot allow the number of theories, designs and alternatives to swamp our decisions about kids' rooms. This smorgasbord of choices is really quite necessary. It attests to the innumerable varieties of family life.

For some families, the children's room is meant to be a total environment, an almost Victorian nursery in which to play, sleep, read, work, study and eat. The TV and stereo have replaced the Nanny, but these neo-Victorian rooms cry out, "Come in, stay home, don't leave!" Thus, some parents favor their children to be off by themselves in their own wing of the house, allowing the rest of the household the peace and quiet of civilized adulthood. In other families, the kids' room is equipped primarily for sleep and little else. Play, study, recreation and meals are communal rituals, involving the entire family, occurring in big family rooms or rec rooms, the fusion of generations and almost total disregard for age differences similar to the family life we might have found in a medieval peasant's one-room cottage or the traditional longhouse of the Iroquois tribes.

Ultimately, space and money determine much of what a child's room will look like, overriding parental preferences regarding which activities of the day are for family sharing and which are for segregating the family by sex or age into specialized rooms. A cramped urban apartment in a neighborhood with few (or no) outdoor playgrounds may have to accommodate, in a small room, the recreational space that suburban kids with sprawling yards and parks find outdoors. Parents with a small urban home and a modest income must utilize limited space, in an exceptionally ingenious way to meet a child's many needs, while more affluent parents in a rambling residential neighborhood may have the luxury of spacious rooms for their children.

Yet even within the constrictions that space and money impose, parents silently communicate to their children their expectations about family life by their choice of furniture, wall color, floor design and bedspread material. In countless ways, the decor and arrangement of a kid's room announces what is important.

We never realized it as children, but architects have traditionally considered kids' rooms to be "secondary rooms" in the total design of the house. Not as important as the living room or kitchen or what we later found out was called the "master bedroom." Not important, they thought, the architects who understand angles! How little they knew! Our room was one of the most important places during those childhood years of growing up. What is more, we knew instinctively the "primary places" in those so-called "secondary rooms," places even parents probably ranked as less important: the floor, the ceiling, and the bottom four feet of wall space.

As toddlers and preschoolers, we preferred the floor to furniture, a cardinal rule of early childhood being that one should never do on a table or bed what can be done on the floor. Play, color, look through magazines, even lie down for a nap: the floor is the spot. And look up at the ceiling. It's too bad there aren't more Michelangelo ceilings in kids' rooms since they spend so much time rolling on the floor and looking up. And when their own muralist instincts consume them in the middle of a boring coloring book, it's too bad the lower regions of the walls are hidden behind furniture. Was it a parental plot to line up the furniture along the reachable areas of the walls?

In planning a room for early childhood, we should make the most of ceiling, floor and lower walls. Even though G.K. Chesterton thought that white ceilings were good in times of illness because kids could lie in bed and pretend they were drawing on them with a long blue pencil, why pretend? Think Baroque, and create a ceiling design so transcendent and extraterrestrial it rivals the nave of a 16th-century church. Spinning hangups overhead help create life and movement also. Kites, mobiles, inflatable animals, even triangular flags conned from a parking lot or gas station attendant can add color, shape and motion to a child's ceiling. Forget the imaginary blue pencil.

When kids are not looking up, they tend to look down. Floor coverings can be patterned after giant checkerboards or yellow brick roads leading under the emerald bed and out of the far side — or simply a wonderland of their favorite cartoon critters. There might even be one spot of washable vinyl so kids can color their own designs. There is some controversy over soft and hard floors for crawlers, scooters and toddlers. Certainly, carpeting is softer, warmer, absorbs more noise, and provides a safer pad for crash landings, but some carpeting material is hard to keep clean when paints, crayons, milk and Silly Putty mysteriously appear ground into the fibers. Perhaps, if the floor area is large enough, there might be both hard and soft places.

As parents, we should get down and crawl from time to time so we can experience both the irresistible urge to draw on the walls and the elfin view from three feet. Scrubbable vinyl wall paneling, a slate liner or chalkboard along the base of one wall creates an official place to indulge one's passion for murals. The other walls could be papered, painted, or stretched with fabric, preferably in bright colors and shapes since children, even babies, react to bright primary colors better than the flamingo pinks and bird's-egg blues that parents have traditionally thought appropriate for their infants' nests.

For the first seven or eight years of their lives, children do not distinguish play from work very well. In fact, they work hard at playing, precisely because it is their main avenue to knowledge and maturity. Much of this "play – work" time will be in their rooms. Toys are, in some sense, tools and should be kept handy. Storage problems can be alleviated if there are lots of open shelves, easily accessible to small hands and eyes. When kept in view, favorite toys are constant reminders and invitations to keep active. Besides, kids are proud to display their treasures and feel more secure with them around. Nothing retards spontaneity more than favorite dolls and stuffed animals hidden in drawers or trunks too heavy to open. The easier it is for children to play and relax in their rooms, the better because, in the long, long hours of childhood, relaxation and leisurely fooling around is the playground of discovery, revealing the mysteries of themselves and of the physical world around them.

As children move into their grade-school years, a number of transformations take place in their rooms. For one, the earlier decor begins to look "babyish" and must be changed. Second, they learn, sadly, that not all work is play, a cruel discovery usually made over homework. Third, a younger brother or sister may have arrived and the private bedroom must now be shared. So for a number of reasons, a child's room needs change. Wise parents realize the growing need of the child to put his or her stamp on the room and will not turn the new room into a showcase for their own lost fantasies. Kids wants to have some say in the new decor. Whatever combination of parent-child motifs is arrived at, it is best not to overprogram a child's room to the exclusion of other reveries. A bedroom that is excessively nautical, princesslike or cowboy-style can crowd out alternative daydreams. Children at this age tend to grow tired of things quickly anyway, so a flexible grade schooler's room should be open-ended enough in color and character to allow fierce rearranging of furniture and fantasies.

Work. Homework. Children need their first serious study area when they begin to get homework; usually a desk in a quiet, well-lit corner of the room will do. Also very important is a large enough work space for them to leave out books, clay, glue, construction paper, pencils and things they're working on, whether it be for a school project or a hobby in progress. In addition, the squirrely instinct that transforms kids into collectors will require shelves and display areas for assemblages of dolls, seashells, model automobiles or dinosaurs. Even though the distinction between work and play becomes sharper, many kids genuinely enjoy doing homework and fiddling with their personal hobbies. Desk and work tables, therefore, acquire a warm, emotional dimension to them that parents sometime overlook in the clutter. Kids need to safeguard, even from us, the little corners of the world where they keep their talismans and the projects they sleep and breathe.

Frequently, the arch-intruder is a little brother or sister. Converting a child's room into "the children's room" requires deft and imaginative planning. There is no hard rule that says a child's room must be a cube tyrannized by six planes. Clever use of bunk beds, lofts, catwalks, dormer windows and other constructed levels can create several spaces in one room. Room dividers may be bookshelves, modular blocks, even the beds themselves. Area rugs and supergraphics on the walls can create the illusion of separate territories, giving each child a sense of personal space in a shared room. As children grow, and more of them come, buying a furniture "system," rather than odd pieces here and there, gives the room a coherent look and can prevent one child from feeling slighted by some real or imagined shortcoming in his or her pieces of furniture.

Good lighting is essential for children. In general, kids require more light than adults during the years when their vision can be impaired by close-scrutiny work over the square roots of imaginary numbers and the faded dates in their coin collections. Children respond enthusiastically to variations in lighting to match their variable moods. A quiet reading area uses a different lighting scheme than the play area. Track lights, floor lamps, overhead fixtures, and desk lamps allow a child to find his or her spot in the room to suit the mood or activity and so distinguish it from whatever the rival sibling might be up to in the same room.

In addition to artificial lighting, a great kids' room exploits natural lighting to the best possible advantage. Incomparable assets in any room are windows and skylights. Blinds, curtains, shades and shutters, if properly utilized, can determine the amount of light that filters into the children's room, allowing the daily path of the sun to alter the lighting effect on the floor, across the bed, in the corners. A prism or piece of stained glass located near a window can splay a veritable rainbow of moving colors through the room. Easy access to the windowsill should not be hampered, particularly if the view is a good one. Children can spend many whimsical moments dreaming at the window on inclement days or, in the evening before they fall asleep, watching the lights come on in their friends' homes, fireflies blink on and off in the yard, the last night birds swoop in the dimming sky above the rooftops.

When a family's children reach their teens, the need for more rooms becomes acute. A teenager desires more privacy in this last period of living at home, in the transitional years when the body and the personal sense of self are neither child nor adult. A teenager's room, if it is private, will usually become more than just a bedroom. It may acquire the look of a sitting room or even a studio apartment. The furniture collected during these years in fact may leave home with the adolescent and become the first furnishings in his or her apartment or college dorm. If the bedroom will not suffice, or if it must be shared with younger gremlins, the attic or basement — the two most-often-wasted areas of the house — can be remodeled into a secondary room for the teenager to listen to music, talk on the phone, hang favorite posters or photomurals, work on hobbies and special projects and, of course, squint into the mirror for long, long hours at a time, noting the most recent changes.

N oise. Always a problem, sometimes bubbling out of the kids' rooms like a creek, other times gushing at floodstage. By adolescence the record player or portable radio have usually become an elaborate and expensive "sound system." A well-planned teenager's room will accommodate both equipment and noise, with extra shelves for records and tapes, perhaps minor rewiring for speakers. Carpets, acoustical tile and redwood paneling all help absorb noise, in addition to creating the soft womblike environment that many teens seek for escape from the family and the ever-growing demands of adult society, a place to gestate for the last time before they are reborn as adults into the world outside their homes and earphones.

However the old room is transformed or the new one added, a teenager should have considerable influence in deciding the decor and arrangement of furniture, even the lock system, in order to put a personal stamp on a personal environment. It is a special place to study, relax, entertain friends and ponder career possibilities. It should be a flexible room, manipulated according to the psychic needs of the season, during the years when their control over their own lives is still awkward and clumsy.

K ids' rooms. Always awkward and clumsy. Spaces we provide for them, spaces they create for themselves. However we hope to arrange them, our own thoughts about rooms are bound to fall short of our children's needs and wills. Comfort, security, stimulation. Yes, they need these; and with corkboard, fabric, wallpaper, carpeting, modular blocks, bedspreads, wooden dressers, map-topped desks and inflatable mice, we can try to construct the perfect room for them. With luck, we might even infuse new life into a room periodically so that it will last for 20 years. But somehow we are destined to fail, especially if our grownup minds, with their short, short thoughts, think only about what we can actually see in their rooms.

We can send our children to their room, but we can never really make them clean it up. For the room they live and play and sleep in is more than the clutter of beds and desks and socks — and dinosaurs spinning from the ceiling — because there is no ceiling. And the view from the window — stretching farther than we can ever hope to see — is the wind's view, and the thoughts of youth are long, long thoughts.

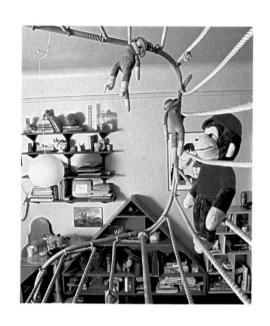

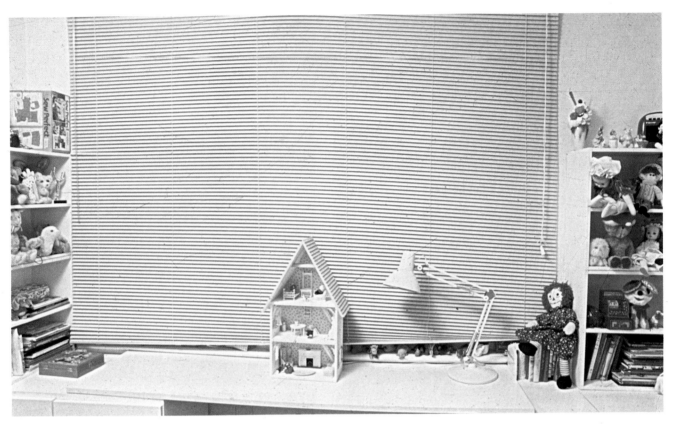

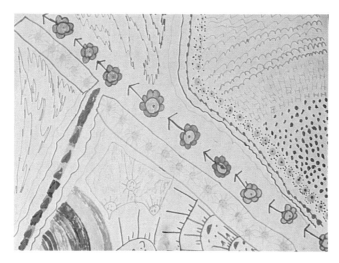

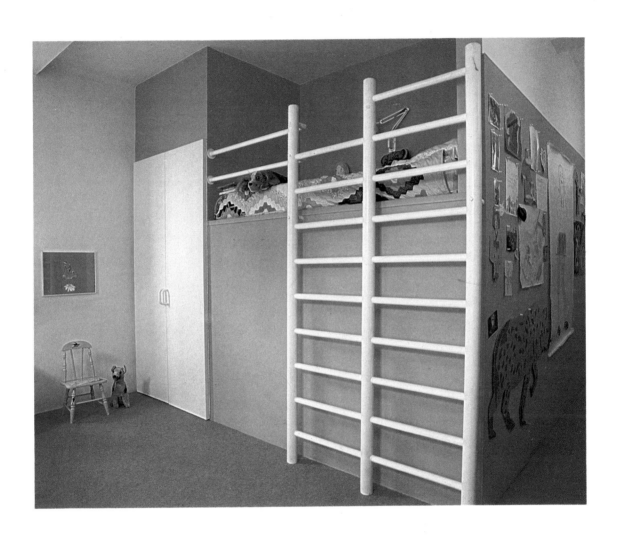